Dan and the Cat

Sounds Easy Series

ISBN 0 905858 70 0

Designed by Howard Birkett,
Amaryllis Software Ltd, Berkhamsted, Herts

Printed by Streetsprinters, Baldock, Herts

Published by
Egon Publishers Ltd
Royston Road, Baldock, Herts SG7 6NW

TEACHERS' NOTES

LEVEL 0. PRE-READING BOOKS

These books have been designed to help children with visual sequential memory difficulties. They draw attention to the vowels 'a', 'o', 'i', 'e' and 'u' (in that order). First say the word to the pupil and talk about the picture. The pupil should then trace each letter with a finger, saying the letter sound at the same time and finally say the whole word. Point out the highlighted vowel.

INTRODUCTORY LEVEL AND LEVEL 1. FIRST READING BOOKS

Can be used as a reading scheme, or as supplementary books to Spelling Made Easy, 'Fat Sam' – Introductory Level and 'Sam and the Tramp' – Level 1 (Violet Brand). They gradually introduce new vowel sounds, reinforcing the word families.

Acknowledgements

Special thanks to John and Heather Adkins, the staff and children of Egerton-Rothesay Lower School, Berkhamsted, to Violet Brand for her encouragement and inspiration and of course to my family, Lucy (for Ted), Joanna (for Top the Frog) and my husband Howard, without whom these books would not have been written.

Dan and the Cat

ROSALIND BIRKETT

Introductory Level Book 1

Sounds Easy Series

EPL

EGON PUBLISHERS LTD

Dan is a man, a fat man.

Dan has a hat and a bag.

Dan the fat man is sad.

A cat sat on his hat.

The cat is fat.

Dan is fat and the cat is fat.